THE
HEART
OF THE
PSALMS
LEADER GUIDE

The Heart of the Psalms
God's Word to the World

The Heart of the Psalms
978-1-7910-4056-7
978-1-7910-4057-4 eBook

The Heart of the Psalms: DVD
978-1-7910-4060-4

The Heart of the Psalms: Leader Guide
978-1-7910-4058-1
978-1-7910-4059-8 eBook

LEADER GUIDE

James C. Howell

——— THE ———
HEART
OF THE
PSALMS
———
GOD'S WORD TO
THE WORLD
———

Abingdon Press | Nashville

The Heart of the Psalms
God's Word to the World
Leader Guide

978-1-7910-4058-1

Cover description for *The Heart of the Psalms: God's Word to the World Leader Guide* by James C. Howell. The title is centered in white and gold text on a textured orange-red background framed in gold and white. At the top, the words *Leader Guide* appearing white within a gold box with a white border. Behind the title panel is Vincent van Gogh's painting *The Starry Night* (1889, oil on canvas). It features a swirling blue and yellow night sky, cypress trees, and a small village with a church steeple.

MANUFACTURED IN THE UNITED STATES OF AMERICA

Contents

Introduction

In *The Heart of the Psalms*, the Rev. Dr. James C. Howell (senior pastor, Myers Park United Methodist Church, Charlotte, North Carolina) invites readers to ponder with him 6 of the 150 psalms in the biblical Psalter. These 6 are his favorite psalms, and he hopes reading, reflecting on, and praying them will lead readers to discover that, as he has, "the Psalms will hack you out of a bogus, simplistic, mechanical, and ultimately disappointing relationship with God, and show you the path to the real thing, tougher, but substantial and life-giving."

This Leader Guide has been written to help you lead a group of adults in a study of James's book and the Psalms, as well as some other Scriptures that he discusses in it. Each of its six session plans corresponds to a chapter in *The Heart of the Psalms*:

- **Session 1: Awe**—Psalm 8 expresses marvel at the majesty of both God the Creator and God's creation. It also gives voice to humility at the honor and the responsibility God has given to the human creature. This session will help participants connect the creative work they are doing and can do with God's own work.

- **Session 2: Beauty**—Psalm 27 contains the psalmist's heartfelt plea to encounter God's holiness and beauty in a world that often confronts us with ugliness and hostility. This session encourages participants to set aside distractions and focus on the few things, or even the one thing, that bring courage and peace.

- **Session 3: Mercy**—Psalm 51 sounds a countercultural but relentlessly honest prayer of confession, exposing human sin to

God's grace. This session gives participants space to consider the practices of confession and testimony in their faith.

- **Session 4: Hope**—Psalm 73 begins in the common but unpleasant emotion of envy but ends in an uncommonly strong affirmation of God's goodness—and perhaps inspired hints about what God promises beyond this life. This session encourages participants to ponder questions of justice and injustice, as well as to reflect on their own hopes for eternal life.

- **Session 5: Time**—Psalm 90 is a sober assessment of how brief our lives are when measured against God's eternity. This session helps participants keep their span of days in proper and godly perspective by reading the psalm against the backdrop of the life of Moses, whom tradition holds was its author.

- **Session 6: Love**—Psalm 116 is a rich declaration of love for God. This session shows participants how calling on God in prayer is an act of loving relationship and ends with the opportunity to practice using language from the psalms in their own prayers.

Although this Leader Guide assumes all participants are reading *The Heart of the Psalms*, its quotations from James's book and inclusion of key Scripture passages mean leaders can also use it on its own. Additionally, the accompanying DVD or streaming video from Amplify Media can supplement these session plans.

Each session contains the following elements to draw from as you plan four in-person, virtual, or hybrid sessions:

- **Session Goals**
- **Biblical Foundation**. Key Scripture texts for each session and quotations from the psalms are from the Revised Standard Version (1952), which James admires for the way it reaches "slightly upward on the quality-of-language scale," as does the original Hebrew. You can use other translations if you prefer, or at least keep others handy for comparison.

- **Before Your Session**. Tips to help you prepare a productive session.
- **Starting Your Session**. Discussion questions intended to "warm up" your group for fruitful discussion.
- **Opening Prayer**. Use the prayer as written or let it suggest a prayer in your own words.
- **Book Discussion Questions**. You likely will not be able or want to use all the questions in every session. Pick and choose questions based on your group's interests and the Spirit's leading.
- **Closing Your Session**. Discussion or reflection focused on a specific quotation from *The Heart of the Psalms*.
- **Closing Prayer**. Each session suggests a hymn that James mentions in the corresponding chapter for use as a closing prayer.

Thank you for your willingness to lead! May you and your group find that your study of these ancient prayers from God's people enriches your own life of prayer and service to God.

Session 1

Psalm 8
Awe: When I Look at the Heavens

Session Goals

This session's reading, reflection, discussion, and prayer will help participants:

- reflect on previous experiences with the Psalms and consider the Psalms' significance in Scripture;
- appreciate the experience of awe expressed in Psalm 8 and connect it to their own experiences of awe;
- consider the psalmist's use of God's name as well as the names they do or don't use for God and why;
- ponder the psalmist's affirmation of God's care for human beings and identify some of its ethical implications; and
- identify a specific way they can use their hands and fingers to share God's care with others.

Biblical Foundation

O LORD, our Lord,
how majestic is thy name in all the earth!

Thou whose glory above the heavens is chanted
  by the mouth of babes and infants,
thou hast founded a bulwark because of thy foes,
  to still the enemy and the avenger.

When I look at thy heavens, the work of thy fingers,
  the moon and the stars which thou hast established;
what is man that thou art mindful of him,
  and the son of man that thou dost care for him?

Yet thou hast made him little less than God,
  and dost crown him with glory and honor.

Psalm 8:1-5

Then Moses said to God, "If I come to the people of Israel and say to them,
'The God of your fathers has sent me to you,' and they ask me, 'What is his
name?' what shall I say to them?" God said to Moses, "I AM WHO I AM."
And he said, "Say this to the people of Israel, 'I AM has sent me to you.'"
God also said to Moses, "Say this to the people of Israel, 'The LORD, the
God of your fathers, the God of Abraham, the God of Isaac, and the God
of Jacob, has sent me to you': this is my name for ever, and thus I am to be
remembered throughout all generations."

Exodus 3:13-15

Before Your Session

- Carefully and prayerfully read Psalm 8 and this session's Biblical
  Foundation more than once. Note words and phrases that attract
  your attention and meditate on them. Write down questions
  you have and try to answer them, consulting trusted Bible
  commentaries.

- Carefully read the introduction and chapter 1 of *The Heart of the Psalms* more than once.
- You will need either Bibles for in-person participants (*optional*: of the same translation, for unison reading) or screen slides prepared with Scripture texts for sharing (identify the translation used), or both; newsprint or a markerboard and markers (for in-person sessions); paper, pens or pencils (in-person).
- If using the DVD or streaming video, preview the session 1 video segment. Choose the best time in your session plan for viewing it.
- *Optional*: hymnals/songbooks used in your congregation; images from either the James Webb Space Telescope (https://science .nasa.gov/mission/webb/multimedia/images/) or Hubble Space Telescope (https://science.nasa.gov/mission/hubble/multimedia /hubble-images/), or both; recording of the song "From a Distance" (Julie Gold, 1985; covered by Bette Midler, 1990) for the section "Why Bother with Us?"

Starting Your Session

Welcome participants. Express why you are enthusiastic about leading this study of *The Heart of the Psalms*. Invite participants to talk briefly about what they hope to gain from the study.

Invite participants to turn in their Bibles to and spend a few minutes browsing the Psalms. Encourage them to call out what catches their attention—words, phrases, images, or numbers of psalms they recognize. Discuss:

- How familiar are you with the Psalms? Why?
- James cites Thomas Merton's idea that "God likes it when you have a favorite psalm." If you have a favorite psalm, which one is it, and why?
- How and how often does your congregation use the Psalms in its worship? Why? *Optional*: Look for hymns and songs based on the Psalms in your congregation's hymnal or songbook.

- Why do you think the Psalms are included in the Bible?
- What, if anything, do you think sets the Psalms apart from other poetry, even other religious poetry?
- James suggests the Psalms found their way into Scripture, in part, because God's people "kept collecting and reusing prayers, probably revising and improving them along the way.... [The Psalms were] made sacred by being prayed so long by so many." What prayers, if any, have you or your family collected, reused, and "made sacred," and why?
- James explains Dietrich Bonhoeffer's idea that in the Psalms, we learn God's language for prayer. How have you learned to pray? Are you still learning—and, if so, how? How, if at all, do you distinguish "wishes, hopes, sighs, laments, rejoicings—all of which the heart can do by itself" (Bonhoeffer) from prayer?
- James thinks the psalmists fit author Niall Williams's definition of poets: those who "go deeper" in this world's "terrifying" depths, at "a price." Have you ever prayed in a way you would say had a cost? If so, when? What was the price? If not, would you want to pray in the deep way the psalmists prayed? Why or why not?

Read aloud from James's book: "The Psalms will hack you out of a bogus, simplistic, mechanical, and ultimately disappointing relationship with God, and show you the path to the real thing, tougher, but substantial and life-giving." Tell participants this study will explore six of James's favorite psalms in the hope of nourishing a more authentic relationship with God.

Opening Prayer

Eternal God, you have always called your people to sing out to you. In joy and in sorrow, in health and in sickness, in anger and in peace, in times of fear and times of hope—always, you long to hear your people's songs, and always, you sing back your own song of presence and love. By your Spirit, help us hear and respond to your voice as we study these Psalms, that we may raise our voices more fully and faithfully in the service of your Word, your song, made flesh, Jesus Christ. Amen.

Watch Session Video

Watch the session 1 video segment together. Discuss:

- Which of James's statements most interested, intrigued, surprised, or confused you? Why?
- What questions does this video segment raise for you?

Awe

Discuss:

- What is awe? When did you last experience it?

Invite one participant to read Psalm 8 aloud while other participants listen *without* following along silently. After the reading, ask participants what words, phrases, or images most captured their attention. Write their responses on newsprint or markerboard. *Optional*: Instead of using a single reader, provide all participants with the same translation and read Psalm 8 aloud in unison; or invite two participants to read the psalm from two different translations, one after the other.

Optional: Display images from the space telescopes during this portion of your session.

Discuss:

- How often do you spend time outside at night? Do you enjoy it? Why or why not?
- Have you ever experienced awe looking at the night sky? Why do you think so many people do?
- Why does seeing "the moon and the stars" (verse 3b) inspire awe in the psalmist?

- Do scientific insights into the "heavens" decrease or increase appreciation of them as God's "work" (verse 3a)? Why?
- "Awe, perhaps especially of the night sky, has curative powers." When, if ever, have you experienced awe as healing?
- What, if anything, do you make of the fact that, as James notes, Psalm 8 occurs "in the middle of a thicket of ten complaint psalms" (Psalms 3–13)?
- James notes the Hebrew verb translated "look at" (verse 3a; *'ereh*) is "'see,' 'consider,' 'gaze'—or 'ponder.'" What's the distinction? What do you take time to "ponder" and why?
- "Awe takes time; it demands that we are still and curious." How, if at all, do you cultivate time for awe in your life?
- "Awe is humanity's most precious ability." Do you agree? Do you think it is, as James suggests it might be, "part of our being created in God's image"? Why or why not?

The Name of Our Lord

Recruit a volunteer to read aloud Exodus 3:13-15. Discuss:

- What do or would you describe as "majestic"?
- What does calling God's name "majestic" mean (Psalm 8:1)?
- As James notes, the psalmist first addresses God as YHWH (probably pronounced "Yahweh"; read aloud as "Adonai," "my Lord," by observant Jews; often rendered in English Bibles as "Lord"), the name God reveals to Moses in Exodus 3. Why does Moses want to know God's name?
- James says God's answer "is either no explanation at all or a singularly spectacular, mysterious, and ultimately truthful explanation." How do you understand the name that God reveals to Moses?
- James explains that YHWH "is a verb...in motion...[causing] things—all things!—to happen...[and] future tense." Do these qualities apply to God as you have experienced God? Why or why not?

- "There are so many names for God in Scripture—as is fitting, God being God, God's being so large and mysterious and complex." What biblical name(s) for God do you find most meaningful? Why? What other names for God, if any, do you use, and why?
- Some people object to "Lord" as a name for God because of its masculine nature and its associations with power. What do you think? What traditional or widely accepted names for God, if any, do you avoid using, and why?
- How does Psalm 8's presentation of God reinforce or challenge traditional ideas of lordship?
- The psalmist also addresses YHWH, "LORD," as "our Lord" ("our Sovereign," NRSVue). How important is the distinction between addressing God as "the Lord" or "my Lord," and "our Lord"? How does (or how should) each address shape the way we live?

Why Bother with Us?

Recruit a volunteer to read aloud again Psalm 8:3-8. Discuss:

- When is a time you remember feeling especially small, as the psalmist feels?
- James thinks the psalmist also feels lonely and insignificant. How do you deal with those feelings when you have them?
- What is God's attitude toward human beings, according to the psalmist? To what evidence of God's attitude does the psalmist point? What evidence for or against the psalmist's conclusion would you point to and why?
- What do you think is lost or gained by translating verse 4—which uses individual masculine nouns from the Hebrew ("man," "the son of man")—with plural, more inclusive nouns ("humans," "mortals," NRSVue)?
- What does it mean for humanity to have "dominion" over God's works (verse 6a)? Do you understand humanity's place in the natural world as the psalmist does? Why or why not?

- James calls Psalm 8 "aspirational" and a "dream in the night." How can and does it offer hope to people who feel lost and alone in darkness, literal or otherwise?

- James states the psalmist's ability to raise the question of God's concern for humanity is a "lovely gift.... It doesn't occur to cockroaches and squirrels to ask.... Even [people] who aren't very spiritual or religious wonder about belonging in the universe." Do you agree? Why or why not?

- Listen to the song "From a Distance." How does it resonate with and differ from Psalm 8? What do you think God feels when God looks on humanity and the world, and why?

- "To know I am small, vulnerable, and dependent is the opening to healing from God and among others." When and how, if ever, has knowledge of your own smallness opened you to healing?

- James says Psalm 8 "starts so very big... [then] escorts us to a very small place, to meet and connect with a God who comes low enough and small enough to embrace us." Have you ever felt God getting low and small enough to embrace you? How? When, if ever, have you offered that embrace of God to someone else?

- How do our ideas about the way God views and treats humanity influence and form the ways we view and treat one another?

Closing Your Session: God's Fingers and Ours

Read aloud from *The Heart of the Psalms*: "There's a single word in Psalm 8 that makes my soul soar. Are you as surprised as I am when you read just past 'When I look at thy heavens' and find 'the work of thy fingers'?... Picturing God with fingers invites us to ponder a God who is personal... and even tender."

Invite participants to spend a few moments looking at and moving their fingers. Discuss:

- What details do you notice most about your fingers?
- "Our fingers do our loveliest work," writes James. What lovely work do you do or have you done using your fingers?
- James points out your first embrace was likely your embrace of a parent's fingers when you were born. How do "babes and infants" "chant" God's glory (Psalm 8:2)? How can a baby's grasp point us toward God?
- James states Psalm 8 is not a prediction of Jesus but still finds a "subtle tease" of God's becoming human in Jesus in the psalmist's mention of "the son of man" (verse 4b). How did Jesus use his hands and his fingers to reveal God with us as one of us in him?
- James quotes Mother Teresa: "What we do is nothing but a drop in the ocean. But if we didn't do it, the ocean would be one drop less." What is one "drop" you will do with your hands and fingers to share God's care before our next session?

Optional: Encourage participants to bring with them to your next session a picture of beauty. You might also have participants send their images to you electronically ahead of time so you can display their pictures in a slideshow.

Closing Prayer

Sing or read together "Creating God, Your Fingers Trace" (*The United Methodist Hymnal* 109; https://hymnary.org/text/creating_god_your _fingers_trace) or another hymn or song based on or inspired by Psalm 8.

Psalm 27
Beauty: One Thing Have I Asked

Session Goals

This session's reading, reflection, discussion, and prayer will help participants:

- think about and share examples of beauty;
- reflect on the psalmist's request to behold God's beauty (Psalm 27:4) and times they themselves have beheld God's beauty;
- consider the significance of the temple in the faith of ancient Israel and the significance of houses of worship in their own lives;
- ponder whether and how they have experienced beauty in Christ and in Christ's Body in the world today; and
- apply Jesus's encouragement to Martha to focus on the "few things" or "one" thing needed (Luke 10:38-42) in their lives.

Biblical Foundation

The LORD is my light and my salvation;
whom shall I fear?

The LORD is the stronghold of my life;
  of whom shall I be afraid?

When evildoers assail me,
  uttering slanders against me,
my adversaries and foes,
  they shall stumble and fall.

Though a host encamp against me,
  my heart shall not fear;
though war arise against me,
  yet I will be confident.

One thing have I asked of the LORD,
  that will I seek after;
that I may dwell in the house of the LORD
  all the days of my life,
to behold the beauty of the LORD,
  and to inquire in his temple.

Psalm 27:1-4

Now as [Jesus and the disciples] went on their way, he entered a village; and a woman named Martha received him into her house. And she had a sister called Mary, who sat at the Lord's feet and listened to his teaching. But Martha was distracted with much serving; and she went to him and said, "Lord, do you not care that my sister has left me to serve alone? Tell her then to help me." But the Lord answered her, "Martha, Martha, you are anxious and troubled about many things; one thing is needful. Mary has chosen the good portion, which shall not be taken away from her."

Luke 10:38-42

Before Your Session

- Carefully and prayerfully read Psalm 27 and this session's Biblical Foundation more than once. Note words and phrases that attract your attention and meditate on them. Write down questions you have and try to answer them, consulting trusted Bible commentaries.

- Carefully read chapter 2 of *The Heart of the Psalms* more than once.
- You will need either Bibles for in-person participants (*optional*: of the same translation, for unison reading) or screen slides prepared with Scripture texts for sharing (identify the translation used), or both; newsprint or a markerboard and markers (for in-person sessions); paper, pens or pencils (in-person).
- If using the DVD or streaming video, preview the session 2 video segment. Choose the best time in your session plan for viewing it.
- *Optional*: If you asked participants to send pictures of beauty to you ahead of time, prepare a digital slideshow of those pictures to show during the session.
- *Optional*: Prepare a digital slideshow of images of houses of worship in a variety of styles and from a variety of places and time periods. Include old pictures of your congregation's building, if applicable and available.

Starting Your Session

Welcome participants. If you asked them to bring pictures of beauty with them or if you have prepared a slideshow using their contributions, take time now to look at and enjoy one another's images together.

Discuss:

- What is beauty?
- Which of our senses can perceive beauty?
- How easy or difficult is it for you to perceive beauty in your everyday life? Why?
- James writes, "You can only 'behold' beauty—not 'hold' but 'behold.'" What's the distinction? Do you agree? Why or why not?
- "The spiritual life could be defined as a long training in learning to notice beauty we've been missing." How, if at all, do you think your faith and spirituality influence your ability to notice and appreciate beauty?

- "God could have made a functional world without [beauty], and we wouldn't even know what we'd been missing." Are function and beauty always or often at odds? Why?
- "There's some moral demand in beauty," James suggests, that "inspires us to act in beautiful ways." When, if ever, has beholding beauty inspired you to act in a beautiful way? What happened?
- James also suggests there is mercy in beauty: "There is so much ugliness out there, even in our own heads and hearts." When was a time you have experienced beauty as mercy?
- James states, "We are responsible to preserve beauty." What do you do to preserve beauty? Why have you chosen that particular beauty to preserve?

Read aloud from *The Heart of the Psalms*: "How good of God to dazzle us with so much beauty.... We are made for beauty.... Beauty ushers us very close to the mind and heart of God." Tell participants that, in this session, your group will explore the yearning and hope for God's beauty found in Psalm 27.

Opening Prayer

God Most High and Holy, we praise you for all the beauty we can experience in this world and in our lives—breathtaking, spectacular, humble, or fleeting. As we turn again to the ancient songs of your people, may your Spirit reveal your beauty to us. Help us grow better able to perceive, appreciate, preserve, and rejoice in true beauty wherever we find it, knowing it is all a gift from you. We ask in the name of the one who is the reflection of your glory and the exact imprint of your very being, Jesus Christ. Amen.

Watch Session Video

Watch the session 2 video segment together. Discuss:

- Which of James's statements most interested, intrigued, surprised, or confused you? Why?

- What questions does this video segment raise for you?

"One Thing Have I Asked"

Invite one participant to read Psalm 27 aloud while other participants listen, *without* reading along silently. After the reading, ask participants what words, phrases, or images most captured their attention. Write their responses on newsprint or markerboard. *Optional*: Instead of using a single reader, provide all participants with the same translation and read Psalm 27 aloud in unison; or invite two participants to read the psalm from two different translations, one after the other.

After the reading, discuss:

- Psalm 27 includes an important mention of beauty, but in James's words, "Notice all the stress and terror in the verses leading up to and following Psalm 27:4!" What problems and dangers is the psalmist facing? How much or how little can you relate to these experiences and why?
- How would you explain the relationship of Psalm 27:4 to the rest of the psalm? How do you characterize the psalm's overall tone?
- "The 'one thing' our psalmist seeks isn't just to behold beauty, as noble and healing as that clearly can be, but 'to behold the beauty of the Lord.'" What is the distinction between the two? How, if at all, do beauty and "the beauty of the Lord" relate to each other?
- James points out that though the psalmist asks for "one thing," "it's really two or three." What are the specific parts of the psalmist's request in verse 4—and how might these "two or three" things all be seen as "one thing" after all?
- "Psalm 27 illustrates how the individual discovers true individuality by being part of the community, especially in prayer." When and how has your community helped you see beauty? When and how has it helped you see God's beauty?

Inquiries in God's Temple(s)

Point out the psalmist's mention of the temple in Psalm 27:4. Discuss:

- Why was the temple in Jerusalem significant to ancient Israel? (1 Kings 8; Psalm 84)
- "The visible manifestation of the Lord's beauty, for the ancient Israelites, was the temple.... Worship in that temple was designed to induce awe and praise for the Lord whose house it was." Skim 1 Kings 6. What details about the temple impress you as most beautiful or awe-inspiring?
- "The Israelites associated God's glory with brightness," writes James, and the temple architects "knew how to exploit light to heighten the beauty of the place, inside and out." Why does Scripture associate God with light? How effective or appropriate an image for God do you find light to be, and why?
- Before the temple, during their wilderness wanderings, the Israelites worshiped God in a movable tabernacle (tent) decorated with Egyptian treasure they had taken with them when leaving slavery (Exodus 12:35-36). James asks whether "whatever precious items we've accrued could glorify God best not worn around our necks or dangling from our ears but by beautifying God's place and furthering the work of God in the world?" What "precious items" would you be willing to give up in these ways, and why? What "precious items" does your congregation use in these ways?
- Read Jeremiah 7:1-11. How do the prophet's words expose temptations and dangers in associating God with any one particular place, even one so beautiful as the temple? How do such temptations and dangers face people of faith today?
- The psalmist speaks of his desire "to inquire" in the temple (Psalm 27:4c). When and how can inquiry be a beautiful act of worship? What inquiries have you made or do you make in worship?

Optional: Display the images of houses of worship that you collected before the session.

- James says that, when he travels, he "always take[s] note of the churches and tr[ies] to pause and offer a prayer of thanksgiving." How often do you note or have you noted churches and other houses of worship when traveling? Do you make a point of going to worship when you are traveling? Why or why not?

- "Church spires are no longer the tallest structures in our cities, but even in the shadows of skyscrapers, they do bear witness that there still is a God." What specific church building(s), if any, bears an especially strong witness to God, in your eyes? Why?

- Which architectural features, if any, about your congregation's building do you think glorify God and why?

- James quotes Frederick Buechner's suggestion that the church might benefit from having its buildings (among much else) swept away, because then "all we would have left would be each other and Christ, which was all there was in the first place." Do you think buildings mostly help or hinder the church today? Why? How is your congregation's building (if it has one) either a burden or a blessing, or both, in your service to God and neighbor?

- In medieval cathedrals, James writes, some of the most beautiful works of art are out of human sight, "exclusively for God." How much value do you think art created and displayed solely for the divine audience has, and why?

- James tells of a woman who faithfully attended worship even when she could no longer hear the service because "in the silence, she found it easier to fix her mind on the Lord." Under what circumstances do you find it easiest to focus on God?

- Read 1 Corinthians 6:19-20. How does or how ought thinking of your body as "a temple of the Holy Spirit" affect how you treat and care for your body?

The Beautiful Body of Christ

- James quotes Fyodor Dostoevsky as claiming only beauty could save the world, and suggesting the only truly beautiful face is Jesus's face. What do you think Dostoevsky meant? Do you imagine Jesus's face as beautiful? Why or why not?
- What do these Scriptures add to a conversation about Jesus's beauty: John 1:1-5, 14; 2 Corinthians 4:6; Colossians 1:15-20?
- Read Isaiah 52:13–53:6. Traditionally, Christians understand this "suffering servant" song as pointing to Jesus. What might it suggest about Jesus's beauty? How can Jesus's suffering train us to find beauty in sorrow and suffering?
- What dangers, if any, accompany looking for beauty in suffering? When and how, if ever, have you tried to bring beauty out of suffering? What happened?
- James calls "God's decision to use the church to be…Christ's literal body" in the world today "a miracle." Do you agree? Why or why not?
- When was a time you have seen the church acting as the beautiful body of Christ? When was a time you have seen it fail to do so?
- How does or could your congregation live even more beautifully as Christ's body?

Closing Your Session: One Thing

Ask participants to silently read Luke 10:38-42. Then read aloud from *The Heart of the Psalms*: "Mary was beholding the beauty of the Lord; she was inquiring in the temple that he was. The speaker in Psalm 27 was distracted by many troubles. Could it be that really just one thing is needful for him, for Martha, for us?"

Discuss:

- What tone of voice do you imagine Jesus using with Martha? Why?

- What "many things" distracted Martha from focusing on the "few things needed—indeed only one" (verses 41-42)? What are the few things or one thing about which Jesus is speaking?
- How do you imagine Martha responded to Jesus? Why?
- James says he has known people "who manage a peaceful and even joyful orientation even in the thick of racket or crises or hurry or weariness." Have you known such people? If so, who? How did they come by that orientation?
- What do you do when you "are anxious and troubled about many things"? What is one specific way you can choose "the better part" in those circumstances?

Lead participants in praying the final verse of Psalm 27 as a breath prayer: As you read "Be strong, and let your heart take courage," participants deeply inhale; as you read "Yea, wait for the Lord!" participants slowly exhale. Repeat several times, allowing several different participants to lead the prayer.

Closing Prayer

Sing or read together "Fairest Lord Jesus" (*The United Methodist Hymnal* 189; https://hymnary.org/text/fairest_lord_jesus_ruler_of_all_nature) or a hymn or song based on or inspired by Psalm 27.

Session 3

Psalm 51
Mercy: Create in Me a Clean Heart

Session Goals

This session's reading, reflection, discussion, and prayer will help participants:

- reflect on their past and current understanding of and ideas about sin;
- explore the concept of mercy, specifically God's mercy, finding examples of it in Scripture and in their own experience;
- consider the story of David's taking of Bathsheba as a possible backdrop to Psalm 51 and for its lessons about sin and sin's consequences;
- think and talk about practices of confession in worship, small groups, and personal relationships; and
- practice giving their testimonies to God's creative activity.

Biblical Foundation

Have mercy on me, O God, according to thy steadfast love;
according to thy abundant mercy blot out my transgressions.

Wash me thoroughly from my iniquity,
and cleanse me from my sin!

For I know my transgressions,
and my sin is ever before me.
Against thee, thee only, have I sinned,
and done that which is evil in thy sight,
so that thou art justified in thy sentence
and blameless in thy judgment.

. . . .

Fill me with joy and gladness;
let the bones which thou hast broken rejoice.
Hide thy face from my sins,
and blot out all my iniquities.

Create in me a clean heart, O God,
and put a new and right spirit within me.
Cast me not away from thy presence,
and take not thy holy Spirit from me.
Restore to me the joy of thy salvation,
and uphold me with a willing spirit.

Psalm 51:1-4, 8-12

Before Your Session

- Carefully and prayerfully read Psalm 51 and this session's Biblical Foundation more than once. Note words and phrases that attract your attention and meditate on them. Write down questions you have and try to answer them, consulting trusted Bible commentaries.
- Carefully read chapter 3 of *The Heart of the Psalms* more than once.
- You will need either Bibles for in-person participants (*optional*: of the same translation, for unison reading) or screen slides prepared with Scripture texts for sharing (identify the translation used), or both; newsprint or a markerboard and markers (for in-person sessions); paper, pens or pencils (in-person).

- If using the DVD or streaming video, preview the session 3 video segment. Choose the best time in your session plan for viewing it.
- *Optional*: Recruit several readers to prepare a reading of 2 Samuel 11:1–12:15, taking the roles of the narrator, David, Bathsheba, Uriah, Joab, Nathan, and messengers.

Starting Your Session

Welcome participants. Lead them in brainstorming a list of words, images, and ideas that come to mind when they hear the word *sin*. Write responses on newsprint or markerboard. Discuss:

- How do you define sin? Why?
- How, if at all, have your ideas about sin changed over time?
- When was the last time, if ever, you heard a discussion of sin in a context other than church?
- James cites Karl Menninger's argument in *Whatever Became of Sin?* (1973) that the more science learned about "illness, psychology, heredity, dysfunction, biology, environment, and trauma, sin would gradually cease to be a plausible explanation of why we do and think what we do." Do you think Menninger was correct? Why or why not?
- How much or how little does worship in your congregation talk about sin? Why?
- How can and how has talk of sin hurt people? Does its potential to do damage outweigh any relevance or usefulness it may still possess? Why or why not?
- Do you agree with James's contention that the Seven Deadly Sins now "describe the good life" in the United States? Why or why not?
- "Even churchgoers," writes James, "tend to think, *I'm a pretty good person; I do my best*. We don't come to worship to clear the air and make amends with God. We come to ask for God's help with our

projects or to feel better or for an hour of spiritual entertainment." How much do you agree or disagree with James's assessment and why?

Read aloud from *The Heart of the Psalms*: "God might want us to pray what is *not* in our hearts, or what is contrary to our hearts....If this is so,...Psalm 51, beloved as it is for some of its familiar lines, will require of us some unlearning of what our hearts have absorbed from the culture, and some relearning of old habits of spirituality like the confession of sin, sacrifice, and forgiveness."

Opening Prayer

Righteous and merciful God, in grace you show us the way to live, but we turn aside time and time again—in our own lives, in our communities, and as the human race. We praise you for refusing to abandon us to the ways we choose that lead to death. May your Holy Spirit open our hearts in this time of study to hear you calling us, once more, back to yourself. Move us to respond, trusting not in ourselves but in the one who is himself the Way, the Truth, and the Life, our Savior Jesus Christ. Amen.

Watch Session Video

Watch the session 3 video segment together. Discuss:

- Which of James's statements most interested, intrigued, surprised, or confused you? Why?
- What questions does this video segment raise for you?

The Quality of Mercy

Invite one participant to read Psalm 51 aloud while other participants listen *without* reading along silently. After the reading, ask participants what words, phrases, or images most captured their attention. Write their responses on newsprint or markerboard. *Optional*: Instead of using a single reader, provide all participants with the same translation and read Psalm 51 aloud in unison; or invite two participants to read the psalm from two different translations, one after the other.

After the reading, discuss:

- What is mercy? How does this psalm help you define or envision mercy?
- On what basis does the psalmist appeal to God for mercy? How would you describe the tone of the psalmist's appeal?
- James discusses two words in the psalm that are translated "mercy": *rachamim*, from *rechem*, "womb"; and *hesed*, "steadfast, unshakably committed love." How do these two Hebrew words influence your understanding of mercy generally? Of God's mercy?
- Read these Scriptures: Exodus 34:6-9; Psalm 86:15-16; 103:8-10; 145:8-9; Nehemiah 9:16-17; Jonah 4:1-2. What do these Scriptures suggest about the importance ancient Israel placed upon God's mercy? How much importance do you place upon God's mercy in your faith?
- "God's mercy is nowhere more brilliantly displayed than when Joseph forgives his vicious brothers and even finds God's hidden hand bringing good out of evil." Read Genesis 45:1-8 and 50:15-20. Although Joseph denies being in God's place (50:19), how is the mercy he shows his brothers like God's mercy? How, if ever, have you seen divine mercy using even "human missteps and meanness for God's good ends," as James suggests?
- Do you agree with James that mercy is "our deepest gut need and our endless quest"? Why or why not?
- How does the psalmist anticipate responding to God's mercy?
- When, if ever, has someone shown you mercy? How did you respond?
- Have you ever been in a position to show mercy to someone? What did you do?

Merciful Commandments?

Ask participants, as a group, to name aloud the Ten Commandments without consulting their Bibles. (The group needn't name them in order!) Write responses on newsprint or markerboard, then check the list against Exodus 20:1-17 and Deuteronomy 5:6-21. Remind participants that while the Ten Commandments aren't an *exhaustive* list of the commandments as in the Torah (God's "law" or "instruction"), they hold an important place in Jewish and Christian ethics. Discuss:

- "The commandments themselves are mercy.... How good of God to show us in mercy the way to a whole, joyful life!" Do you agree? Why or why not?
- Read Exodus 19:1-6. How does this Scripture characterize the nature and purpose of God's commandments?
- Read Matthew 5:21-48. How does Jesus's use of God's commandments seek, in James's words, "to set us free from all that is toxic in our heads and hearts"?
- Quoting James Allison, James suggests sin is "an addiction to being less than ourselves." Do you find addiction a helpful metaphor for sin? Why or why not?
- Commenting on Psalm 51:8b, James writes, "God knows that when we live out of sync with the ways God has mercifully shown us, our bodies sustain damage." How are you aware of sin's damaging physical impact? How does your congregation care for the physical damage people sustain because of their own or others' sin?
- "We dwell in a culture that is not of God, which grieves God's heart. We're enmeshed in it; we share society's troubles." When are you most aware of your own enmeshment in social sin? What do you do about it?

"After He Had Gone in to Bathsheba"

Point out the title (also known as the *superscription*) given to Psalm 51. Review with participants in one of the following ways the story of David's taking of Bathsheba and its aftermath:

- Recruit readers to read aloud 2 Samuel 11:1–12:15 (*optional*: the readers you recruited before the session can present their prepared reading at this point).
- Skim and scan 2 Samuel 11–12 together, having participants point out key events in the story (consider answering the "reporter's questions" of who, what, when, where, why, and how).
- Invite participants to summarize the story in their own words (depending on their biblical knowledge).

Discuss:

- James says this story "will make you blush, and...serves as a diagnosis of what goes awry in all of us and in the people around us." What are your initial reactions to the story? How would you summarize its "diagnosis" of sin?
- James points out the "power differential" in David's behavior toward Bathsheba. Where have you seen before or do you see now similar power differentials happening today? Who are the literal or figurative "kings" today who take whatever they want, and why do they feel they can do so?
- James contrasts David's treatment of Bathsheba with Jesus's treatment of the woman at a well in Samaria (John 4). How does Jesus model respectfully seeing another person *as* a person?
- How and why does David try to cover up what he has done? Have you ever tried and failed to hide wrongdoing? What happened?

- "There is, at the core of God's mercy, an accountability." How does the prophet Nathan hold David accountable to God? Is mercy without accountability true mercy? Why or why not?
- James wonders whether Psalm 51's title "kind of let[s] David off the hook...as if you can sin, and terribly, but if you are eloquently contrite and profoundly emotional in your remorse, all will be well." What do you think?
- What consequences of his sin will David and others his sin affects still have to face? Why doesn't mercy always necessarily involve the avoidance of sin's consequences?
- When, if ever, have you had to deal with the consequences of your own or another's sin, even if that sin was confessed and forgiven? How is your society dealing with the consequences of its past sins?

Confessing What God Already Knows

Discuss:

- "Spiritual growth is about realizing we live our lives on a stage with God as audience." James finds this idea full of mercy. Do you? Why or why not?
- "How odd to confess, to ask, to turn yourself in to God, since God already knows." Do we need to confess sins to God? Why or why not?
- The psalmist says, "I know my transgressions" (Psalm 51:3a). How can confessing our sin make us more aware of it?
- The psalmist says he has sinned against God "only" (verse 4a). Are all sins against others also sins against God? Does confessing sins to God excuse us from confessing them to others? Why or why not?
- James asks, "Does posture matter in confession?" What do you think?

- How, if at all, is confession of sin a part of your congregation's worship? Would you change anything about this part of your worship? Why or why not?
- How can confession create and strengthen community? What risks to community, if any, does confession pose?
- James writes about early Methodists in small groups who regularly confessed their sins to one another. To whom, if anyone, are you accountable for confessing your sin? Who, if anyone, is accountable to you in this way? What benefits and risks does such accountability offer?

Closing Your Session: Testimony

Read aloud from *The Heart of the Psalms*: "The crux of the whole psalm, and the only hope we have, is plain to see in verse 10: 'Create in me a clean heart, O God.'...If God could create a universe, God can craft a whole new heart in you.... Once we begin to live with the newly created heart,...we have a responsibility to tell our story to others.... Testimony is God's best way to reach into the heart of the skeptic, the doubter, and the one who believes he is abandoned by God. Testimony builds community. You narrate what unfolded, how surprised you've been by God."

Discuss:

- James points out that in Scripture, "the Hebrew verb *bara'* [create] [is] never used of anything any human being does." What does this fact tell us about the "clean heart" for which the psalmist prays?
- Whose testimony to God's creative activity in their lives has made a difference to your faith, and how?
- How does your congregation's worship make space for people to share their testimonies to what God has done and is doing for them?
- How comfortable are you giving your own testimony about God's creative activity in your life and in your community? Why?

Invite volunteers who wish to do so to offer a brief testimony to how they have been surprised by what God has created for and in them.

Closing Prayer

Sing or read together "Have Thine Own Way, Lord" (*The United Methodist Hymnal* 382; https://hymnary.org/text/have_thine_own_way _lord) or a hymn or song based on or inspired by Psalm 51.

Session 4

Psalm 73
Hope: For Me It Is Good to Be Near God

Session Goals

This session's reading, reflection, discussion, and prayer will help participants:

- relate their past and present experiences of feeling envy to the psalmist's experience of envy in Psalm 73;
- consider the question of why good people suffer bad things, as well as various responses to that question;
- identify how worship reoriented the psalmist and think about whether and how they have had similar experiences in sacred spaces and among the community of faith;
- reflect on God's past and continuing nearness to humanity in Jesus Christ; and
- ponder how Psalm 73 may offer "inspired hints" about the nature of eternal life, and think about how these insights might shape their view of eternal life.

Biblical Foundation

Truly God is good to the upright,
*   to those who are pure in heart.*
But as for me, my feet had almost stumbled,
*   my steps had well nigh slipped.*
For I was envious of the arrogant,
*   when I saw the prosperity of the wicked.*

. . . .

Behold, these are the wicked;
*   always at ease, they increase in riches.*
All in vain have I kept my heart clean
*   and washed my hands in innocence.*
For all the day long I have been stricken,
*   and chastened every morning.*

If I had said, "I will speak thus,"
*   I would have been untrue to the generation of thy children.*
But when I thought how to understand this,
*   it seemed to me a wearisome task,*
until I went into the sanctuary of God;
*   then I perceived their end.*
Truly thou dost set them in slippery places;
*   thou dost make them fall to ruin.*

. . . .

When my soul was embittered,
*   when I was pricked in heart,*
I was stupid and ignorant,
*   I was like a beast toward thee.*
Nevertheless I am continually with thee;
*   thou dost hold my right hand.*
Thou dost guide me with thy counsel,
*   and afterward thou wilt receive me to glory.*
Whom have I in heaven but thee?
*   And there is nothing upon earth that I desire besides thee.*
My flesh and my heart may fail,
*   but God is the strength of my heart and my portion for ever.*

> For lo, those who are far from thee shall perish;
> thou dost put an end to those who are false to thee.
> But for me it is good to be near God;
> I have made the Lord God my refuge,
> that I may tell of all thy works.
>
> Psalm 73:1-3, 12-18, 21-28

Before Your Session

- Carefully and prayerfully read Psalm 73 more than once. Note words and phrases that attract your attention and meditate on them. Write down questions you have and try to answer them, consulting trusted Bible commentaries.

- Carefully read chapter 4 of *The Heart of the Psalms* more than once.

- You will need Bibles for in-person participants (*optional*: of the same translation, for unison reading) or screen slides prepared with Scripture texts for sharing (identify the translation used), or both; newsprint or a markerboard and markers (for in-person sessions); paper, pens or pencils (in-person).

- If using the DVD or streaming video, preview the session 4 video segment. Choose the best time in your session plan for viewing it.

Starting Your Session

Welcome participants. Tell them that the psalm your group will study today, Psalm 73, begins with a confession of envious feelings. Ask:

- What's your earliest memory of envying someone? For what reason did you envy them?

- Which rich and famous people, past or present, have you envied or do you envy, and why?

- To your knowledge, has anyone ever envied you? Might someone envy you? Why or why not?

- In the last chapter, James mentioned the traditional Seven Deadly Sins, of which envy is one. What makes envy a sin? What dangers does it pose to personal relationships? To society? To one's own well-being?
- How do you handle feelings of envy when you have them?

Tell participants that although Psalm 73 begins in envy, it is ultimately about much more. Read aloud from *The Heart of the Psalms*: "[This great text is] a wrestling with God and who God really is, a contest over who you really are and why you're here, and some clues and possibilities about life being more than just this life and what anything beyond might look like."

Opening Prayer

Strong and ever-present God, our true shelter in life's storms and our only sure foundation: May your Spirit guide us today in our reading and reflection, our listening and our speaking, that we might know your ways more fully and tell of your works more faithfully, for the sake and to the glory of our Savior, Jesus Christ. Amen.

Watch Session Video

Watch the session 4 video segment together. Discuss:

- Which of James's statements most interested, intrigued, surprised, or confused you? Why?
- What questions does this video segment raise for you?

Envying the Arrogant

Invite one participant to read Psalm 73 aloud while other participants listen, *without* reading along silently. After the reading, ask participants what words, phrases, or images most captured their attention. Write their responses on newsprint or markerboard. *Optional*: Instead of using a single reader, provide all participants with the same translation and read Psalm 73 aloud in unison; or invite two participants to read the psalm from two different translations, one after the other.

After the reading, discuss:

- What does it mean to be "pure in heart" (verse 1b)? Is being purehearted a prerequisite for experiencing God's goodness? Why or why not?
- James urges readers not to "scurry too quickly past that first word, *surely*." Why do you suppose the psalmist adds this qualifier when declaring God's goodness to the purehearted?
- "But as for me . . . ," says the psalmist (verse 2a). James asks, "What is your 'but'?" What is it that could cause or has caused you to stumble or "almost" stumble in faith?
- James imagines the psalmist had been told not to question or wonder about God. What is your attitude toward questioning God? How has that attitude been shaped?
- The psalmist says "the people turn and praise" those he envies (verse 10a). What do you do when you see people, in James's words, "fawning over the wrong people" today?
- What are the characteristics of those people whom the psalmist envied (verses 3-9)? What might his description of the way he sees them tell us about the way he sees himself?
- Who do you tend to compare and contrast yourself with, and why? To what extent does your faith influence the way you size yourself up against others?

Why Do Bad Things Happen?

Discuss:

- The psalmist wonders if his purity and piety have been "in vain" (verses 13-14). When, if ever, have you wondered or do you wonder whether your own faith and faithfulness are for nothing?

- In this chapter of his book, James tells the story of his friend Thaniel's death, and asks, "Don't we all know people who are extraordinarily good and holy but who suffer awfully?" Whom have you known who fits this description?
- James mentions some commonly heard answers to the question "Why do bad things happen to good people?" How helpful or unhelpful, faithful or unfaithful, do you find each of these responses, and why?
  ◊ "God's in control."
  ◊ "God won't give you more than you can handle."
  ◊ Suggestions that suffering is somehow for the best (e.g., "He's in a better place").
- How do *you* answer the question of why good people suffer? Would you or do you answer this question differently in different situations? Why or why not?
- "In the face of suffering, you can be present, and it's best while present simply to be silent." What makes silence so valuable when with someone who is suffering? When, if ever, has another person's silence in the face of your suffering helped you? When, if ever, is silence *not* helpful or valuable when others suffer?
- Why do you think Psalm 73 offers no answer to the question of why the psalmist is suffering?

Reorientation in the Sanctuary and the Community

Discuss:

- James calls verse 17 "the turning point, the major twist in [the] plot" of Psalm 73. Why? How is what comes after verse 17 different from what came before?
- For ancient Israel, "the sanctuary of God" was the temple in Jerusalem. Where is "the sanctuary of God" for you—a place

you consider "mystically alive, even on fire, with the presence of God"—and why?

- Israelites came to the temple, writes James, "seeking blessing and mercy but often got far more." Read Isaiah 6:1-8, which James cites as one example. How was Isaiah reoriented in that sanctuary of God? When, if ever, has an experience in worship reoriented you in some way?

- James suggests the psalmist's reorientation in the sanctuary anticipates Jesus's story of the prodigal son, who "came to himself" (Luke 15:17; "came to his senses," NRSVue). What connections can you make between Psalm 73 and the parable? When was a time you "came to yourself," and what happened as a result?

- "God wants us to show up, simply to be there, and to be present." How do you make yourself present to God?

- "The psalmist's change of heart resulted from sanctuary and community." When and among whom are you most aware of God's presence? Why?

- When and how, if ever, has the community of God's children (verse 15) helped you, in James's words, "to believe, to survive dark days, and to cling to God when God seems absent"?

- "Invisibly but surely, even the saints who have died hover in the sanctuary and envelop us with love, faith, and power." Who are some of these hovering saints for you and your congregation? How is their presence still felt in your congregation's life together?

- James says he finds himself "wishing the psalmist had kept verses 18-20 to himself." Do you agree? How, if at all, can we square the psalmist's sudden conviction about the "end" of the wicked with his sense of being close to God?

- James hopes the psalmist eventually recognized "that [his enemies'] only hope is the same as his—in discovering God's nearness." How easy or difficult do you find it to believe God is as near to your enemies, or those you regard as your enemies, as God is near to you? Why?

God Gives God's Self

Discuss:

- "We talk too loosely about God's blessings," James states. Do you agree? Why or why not? How can talk of "blessings" confuse others, or we ourselves, about what and how God gives?
- The psalmist declares he desires nothing but God (verse 25). How much or how little do you relate to this desire? Why?
- "The 'good' that God gives isn't this or that tangible reward.... God is the good.... What God gives is God's own self." When, if ever, have you experienced God's presence as a good in your life, apart from specific good things?
- James suggests the psalmist's realization of God's nearness anticipates God coming near humanity in Jesus: "No wonder God thought the best possible nickname for Jesus would be Immanuel." How was Jesus "God with us" during his earthly ministry? How is Jesus, no longer on the earth, still "God with us" today?
- James writes that, in Jesus, "God engages in stunning solidarity with us" by taking our suffering "onto the divine heart." How does Jesus's suffering shape your response to your suffering? To others' suffering?
- "God is near, whether we feel it or not, because God promised.... We trust the undeniable fact of God's presence, not our feelings about God's presence or apparent lack thereof." How easy or difficult is it for you to separate your feelings about God's presence from God's promise to be present and why?

Closing Your Session: "Inspired Hints" of Eternal Life

Read aloud again Psalm 73:23-26. Discuss:

- What do you think the psalmist means when he says God will "afterward... receive [him] to glory" (verse 24b)?

- Commenting on verse 24, James writes, "Sounds like heaven, but nowhere else in the Bible is heaven spoken of this way!" How much of a role, if any, does "glory" play in your ideas about heaven, or eternal life?

- James wonders if the psalmist, in speaking of God as his "strength" and "portion" "forever" (verse 26b), is making "a tentative venture into the possibility of eternal life," an idea largely absent from the Old Testament. What do you think, and why?

- The psalmist, James suggests, "loves God so much he would grieve death's breaking of the bond," and intuits "that God's love for him is so powerful that God does not wish for it to end either." How much is this image of eternal life like or unlike images you have encountered in the church and in culture? How is it like or unlike your own images of eternal life?

- James asks whether the idea of eternal life hinted at in Psalm 73 might be "the healthiest, most robust and frankly beautiful sense of what eternal life is." How do we determine whether given ideas about eternal life are healthy or unhealthy, robust or weak, ugly or beautiful?

- "The question to ponder is this: Without life after death, would you behave better or worse now?" How do you answer, and why?

Closing Prayer

Sing or read together "O Love That Wilt Not Let Me Go" (*The United Methodist Hymnal* 480; https://hymnary.org/text/o_love_that_wilt_not _let_me_go) or a hymn or song based on or inspired by Psalm 73.

Session 5

Psalm 90
Time: Living with Moses

Session Goals

This session's reading, reflection, discussion, and prayer will help participants:

- review what they know about Moses and consider his life as a backdrop for Psalm 90;
- ponder questions about the purpose of God's law and the relationships between God's wrath and God's mercy raised by Psalm 90 and the story of Moses and the Israelites at Mount Sinai;
- consider the reality of their own and others' mortality, prompted by Psalm 90 and the story of Moses's death on Mount Nebo; and
- reflect on the "work of [their] hands" with which they fill each day.

Biblical Foundation

Lord, thou hast been our dwelling place
  in all generations.
Before the mountains were brought forth,
  or ever thou hadst formed the earth and the world,
  from everlasting to everlasting thou art God.

Thou turnest man back to the dust,
and sayest, "Turn back, O children of men!"
For a thousand years in thy sight
are but as yesterday when it is past,
or as a watch in the night.

. . . .

Who considers the power of thy anger,
and thy wrath according to the fear of thee?
So teach us to number our days
that we may get a heart of wisdom.

. . . .

Let the favor of the Lord our God be upon us,
and establish thou the work of our hands upon us,
yea, the work of our hands establish thou it.
Psalm 90:1-4, 11-12, 17

When Moses came down from Mount Sinai, with the two tables of the testimony in his hand as he came down from the mountain, Moses did not know that the skin of his face shone because he had been talking with God. And when Aaron and all the people of Israel saw Moses, behold, the skin of his face shone, and they were afraid to come near him. But Moses called to them; and Aaron and all the leaders of the congregation returned to him, and Moses talked with them. And afterward all the people of Israel came near, and he gave them in commandment all that the LORD had spoken with him in Mount Sinai.
Exodus 34:29-32

And Moses went up from the plains of Moab to Mount Nebo, to the top of Pisgah, which is opposite Jericho. And the LORD showed him all the land, Gilead as far as Dan....And the LORD said to him, "This is the land of which I swore to Abraham, to Isaac, and to Jacob, 'I will give it to your descendants.' I have let you see it with your eyes, but you shall not go over there." So Moses the servant of the LORD died there in the land of Moab, according to the word of the LORD, and he buried him in the valley in the land of Moab opposite Beth-pe'or; but no man knows the place of his *burial to this day. Moses was a hundred and twenty years old when he died; his eye was not dim, nor his natural force abated.*

Deuteronomy 34:1, 4-7

Before Your Session

- Carefully and prayerfully read Psalm 90 and this session's Biblical Foundation more than once. Note words and phrases that attract your attention and meditate on them. Write down questions you have and try to answer them, consulting trusted Bible commentaries.
- Carefully read chapter 5 of *The Heart of the Psalms* more than once.
- You will need either Bibles for in-person participants (*optional*: of the same translation, for unison reading) or screen slides prepared with Scripture texts for sharing (identify the translation used), or both; newsprint or a markerboard and markers (for in-person sessions); paper, pens or pencils (in-person). *Optional*: Enough soft modeling clay for each participant to have a handful.
- If using the DVD or streaming video, preview the session 5 video segment. Choose the best time in your session plan for viewing it.
- *Optional*: Select several images of Moses—from websites, illustrated Bibles, religious education curriculum, movies and TV—to display at the start of your session. Choose a variety of images from artists of different cultures, ethnicities, and time periods. You may wish to include an image of Michelangelo's statues of Moses, which James discusses in chapter 5.

Starting Your Session

Welcome participants. Lead them in brainstorming a list of everything they know or remember about Moses. Write responses on newsprint or markerboard.

Optional: Display images of Moses gathered before your session and invite participants to react to them. Which one(s) do they most like or dislike, and why? What does each image say (or not say) about Moses? How, if at all, do the images comment on, complement, or contradict one another, and what do these visual interactions suggest?

Discuss:

- If you had to tell in a single sentence who Moses was and why he matters, what would you say?
- What adjectives would you use to describe Moses? Why?
- James notes that Moses's life follows a common biblical pattern: "God surprises someone with a call, not based on a strong resume or profound spirituality.... God overrides every objection, looking not for ability but avail-ability." When has God surprised you by calling you to do something, as God surprised Moses out of the burning bush (Exodus 3:1-6)? What objections, if any, did you raise? Did God override your objections? How?
- What is the most important lesson you think Moses's life offers people today? Why?
- Read aloud from *The Heart of the Psalms*: Psalm 90, "and no other, bears the name of Moses. Mind you, scholars doubt—and for sound reasons—that Moses actually composed it. Even if he didn't...Psalm 90 has everything we know about Moses etched all over it." Tell participants that, in this session, they will explore Psalm 90 in relation not only to Moses's life but also their own.

Opening Prayer

Faithful God, we praise you for your servant Moses, through whom you led your people to freedom and instructed them for a life of liberty. May your Spirit, who rested on and filled him, rest on and fill us now in our study, that we, too, may hear and answer your call to wisely count our days, and to offer our hands, our hearts, and our whole selves for your work. Amen.

Watch Session Video

Watch the session 5 video segment together. Discuss:

- Which of James's statements most interested, intrigued, surprised, or confused you? Why?
- What questions does this video segment raise for you?

Psalm 90 and the Man of Mount Sinai

Invite one participant to read Psalm 90 aloud while other participants listen *without* reading along silently. After the reading, ask participants what words, phrases, or images most captured their attention. Write their responses on newsprint or markerboard. *Optional:* Instead of using a single reader, provide all participants with the same translation and read Psalm 90 aloud in unison; or invite two participants to read the psalm from two different translations, one after the other.

- Based on our discussion so far and on anything else you know about Moses, why do you think, as James writes, "those entrusted with compiling the Psalms into Scripture…attached his name to this one"?
- "Moses was defined less by the wilderness than by mountains." Read Exodus 3:9-12; 19:1-6, 16-20. Why is Mount Sinai, in James's words, "*the* mountain" for Moses and the people of Israel? What connections can you make between Mount Sinai and Psalm 90?
- James reflects that, on top of Mount Sinai, Moses was "more intimate with God than anyone had ever been or would ever be again." When and where have you felt most intimate with God? Do you think Psalm 90 reflects intimacy with God? Why or why not?
- James quotes Zora Neale Hurston's novel *Moses, Man of the Mountain* (1939), which describes the commandments Moses

received on Mount Sinai as "something of the essence of divinity expressed," "the chart and compass of behavior," and laws by which "Israel could be a heaven for all men forever." Do you tend to think of God's law as more of a "rulebook" or an "invitation," in James's words, and why?

- James suggests the consequences we experience when we break away from God's ways "feel like God's wrath—which is what God's mercy feels like to us when it crashes into a wall we've erected instead of being welcomed through an open door." Do you agree with James's explanation of God's wrath? How does it help or not help you understand what this psalm says about God's wrath (verses 7-9)?

- How can God's exposure of our "secret sins" (verse 8b) be a mercy, according to James? When, if ever, have you experienced the exposure of sin as merciful and leading to healing and a fresh start?

- Read Exodus 32:7-35. Moses's first stay with God on Mount Sinai ended when the Israelites made and worshiped a golden calf. How are both human and divine anger and mercy involved in this incident's aftermath? How, if at all, are they connected? What does this story have to say about breaking with God's ways today?

- James notes that Psalm 90 "knits [sin] tightly together with mortality," and that while we ought not think every death is the direct result of sin, "some fair percentage of deaths is in fact due to sin, not just mine but that of humanity." Do you agree? Why or why not?

Psalm 90 and the
Man of Mount Nebo

- Read Deuteronomy 34:1-7. Why is Moses's ascent of Mount Nebo, in James's words, the "second climax (maybe something of an anticlimax)" in Moses's life?

- How do you imagine Moses felt at the top of Mount Nebo? Why?
- The text says Moses died at God's command (verse 5). To what extent do you think, as James states, "the end of each life...rests in God's hands"?
- The text also says Moses remained clear-eyed and vigorous at his death (verse 7). Who is the most clear-eyed and vigorous person in old age you have known?
- "There's no glamour in living long, as the elderly know, bearing their aches and losses." Who is the longest-lived person you have known? What was their attitude toward their longevity?
- What significance, if any, do you find in the unknown location of Moses's grave (verse 6)? Whose grave, if anyone's, do you feel it important to visit and why? Do you think it important that people be able to visit your grave when you are dead? Why or why not?
- "Mortality lurks behind every verse of Psalm 90—as it's always over your shoulder as you go about your business." How would you describe Psalm 90's attention to mortality? How much or little do you think about your own mortality? Others' mortality? Why?
- When was a time you were especially aware of your own mortality? How, if at all, does that experience shape the way you live now?
- Alluding to 1 Thessalonians 4:13, James writes, "We do not grieve as those who have no hope." How important is your faith to you in times of grief? Why?

Closing Your Session:
The Work of Our Hands

Read aloud from *The Heart of the Psalms*: "Our Psalm prays, in fresh hope, 'Establish the work of our hands' (v. 17). Make it matter. Make it endure."

- What adjectives describe "the work of your hands" with which you fill your days?

- James quotes Reinhold Niebuhr: "Nothing that is worth doing can be achieved in our lifetime; therefore we must be saved by hope." What things worth doing are you or have you been involved in that you will not live to see achieved? What motivates and sustains your involvement in these things?
- Psalm 90 prays God will teach us "to number our days that we may get a heart of wisdom" (verse 12). How do you count your days? How do you make each day you are alive count?
- Commenting on the significance of "the morning" (verse 14a), James states that every morning is "a little Easter, a fresh start, and a new creation." How does or how could your morning routine honor God for the gift of each new day?
- Does today's discussion of Psalm 90 and Moses's life lead you to consider other choices about the "work of your hands"? Why or why not?
- How can this community support you as you seek to busy your hands and fill your days with work that God can make matter and endure?

Optional: Distribute a handful of soft modeling clay to each participant. Invite them to mold it into a representation of some "work of their hands" that they pray God will give enduring significance.

Closing Prayer

Sing or read together "O God, Our Help in Ages Past" (*The United Methodist Hymnal* 117; https://hymnary.org/text/our_god_our_help_in _ages_past_watts) or some other hymn or song based on or inspired by Psalm 90.

Session 6

Psalm 116
Love: Precious in the Sight of the Lord

Session Goals

This session's reading, reflection, discussion, and prayer will help participants:

- become more familiar with Psalms 113–118, the psalms appointed for Passover;
- consider how in Psalm 116 calling on God is an expression of love for God in response to God's own love;
- reflect on the psalmist's experience of being saved from death in light of their own experiences of being near physical and spiritual death;
- make connections between the psalmist's act of thanksgiving, drink offerings in the Old Testament, and Jesus's thanksgiving over the cup at the Last Supper; and
- think about how death may be "precious" in God's sight and in their own.

Biblical Foundation

I love the LORD, because he has heard
    my voice and my supplications.
Because he inclined his ear to me,
    therefore I will call on him as long as I live.

. . . .

Gracious is the LORD, and righteous;
    our God is merciful.
The LORD preserves the simple;
    when I was brought low, he saved me.
Return, O my soul, to your rest;
    for the LORD has dealt bountifully with you.

For thou hast delivered my soul from death,
    my eyes from tears,
    my feet from stumbling;
I walk before the LORD
    in the land of the living.

. . . .

What shall I render to the LORD
    for all his bounty to me?
I will lift up the cup of salvation
    and call on the name of the LORD,
I will pay my vows to the LORD
    in the presence of all his people.
Precious in the sight of the LORD
    is the death of his saints.

Psalm 116:1-2, 5-9, 12-15

Now as they were eating, Jesus took bread, and blessed, and broke it, and gave it to the disciples and said, "Take, eat; this is my body." And he took a cup, and when he had given thanks he gave it to them, saying, "Drink of it, all of you; for this is my blood of the covenant, which is poured out for many for the forgiveness of sins. I tell you I shall not drink again of this fruit of the vine until that day when I drink it new with you in my Father's kingdom."

And when they had sung a hymn, they went out to the Mount of Olives.
Matthew 26:26-30

Before Your Session

- Carefully and prayerfully read Psalm 116 more than once. Note words and phrases that attract your attention and meditate on them. Write down questions you have and try to answer them, consulting trusted Bible commentaries.
- Carefully read chapter 6 of *The Heart of the Psalms* more than once.
- You will need either Bibles for in-person participants (*optional*: of the same translation, for unison reading) or screen slides prepared with Scripture texts for sharing (identify the translation used), or both; newsprint or a markerboard and markers (for in-person sessions); paper, pens or pencils (in-person).
- If using the DVD or streaming video, preview the session 6 video segment. Choose the best time in your session plan for viewing it.

Starting Your Session

Welcome participants. Ask:

- What are your favorite memories of singing with a group?
- What songs do you like to sing or listen to when traveling?
- What are some of your favorite holiday songs (Christmas or another holiday)?

Tell participants that, as James explains in chapter 6, Psalms 113–118 are psalms appointed for Passover, one of three major pilgrimage festivals in Judaism, for which people would travel to Jerusalem to celebrate. (The other two are Shavuot [Pentecost], "Weeks," commemorating God's gift of Torah; and Sukkot, "Booths," thanking God for the harvest and for protecting the Israelites in the Exodus.) The "hymn" Jesus and his disciples sang after their Passover meal (Matthew 26:30) was likely one of these psalms.

Have participants turn to Psalms 113–118 in their Bibles and spend some time skimming these psalms. Ask:

- What words or images from these psalms most capture your attention? Why?
- What similarities among these psalms do you notice?
- Why are these psalms particularly associated with or appropriate for Passover?
- What language and images from these psalms make you think of Jesus and why?

Tell participants that in this session they will explore one of these psalms, Psalm 116, in more detail.

Opening Prayer

Loving God, we cannot catalog or count all the ways you have dealt bountifully with us, let alone offer thanksgiving enough. Yet in your goodness you welcome our gratitude, feeble and faltering though it is. Even more, you yearn for our love. May our Spirit so fill our minds and hearts in these moments of study that they become our grateful sacrifice to you, a token of our desire to live all our moments in deeper relationship with you. We pray in the name of your greatest gift, your Son, our Savior Jesus Christ. Amen.

Watch Session Video

Watch the session 6 video segment together. Discuss:

- Which of James's statements most interested, intrigued, surprised, or confused you? Why?
- What questions does this video segment raise for you?

"I Love the Lord"

Invite one participant to read Psalm 116 aloud while other participants listen *without* reading along silently. After the reading, ask participants what words, phrases, or images most captured their attention. Write their responses on newsprint or markerboard. *Optional:* Instead of using a single reader, provide all participants with the same translation and read Psalm 116 aloud in unison; or invite two participants to read the psalm from two different translations, one after the other.

After the reading, discuss:

- Why does the psalmist say he loves God (verses 1-2)? What does loving God look like in this psalm?

- James suggests "the God who is love above all else craves just that from us: love." What have you been told God wants from us? From you, specifically? How do you respond to James's assertion that God ultimately wants our love?

- Read Deuteronomy 6:4-9, which contains the Shema (Hebrew, "hear"), "Israel's primal command." What does loving God look like in this passage? How does this passage connect hearing and loving?

- "Love is listening," writes James. "Listening is love." How so? Do you agree?

- According to James, the "quirky" Hebrew grammar of verse 1 opens the possibility that all our loving is possible because God has listened to us. Do you think real love is possible apart from God's love? Why or why not?

- James says many of us only call on God "like a 911 call, when we are in big trouble." Does his statement describe you? Why or why not? How do you think God feels about such "emergency" calls?

- "The Lord wants to hear from us often, daily, constantly, like a real relationship of love." How often do you call on God? Why?

- "The Hebrew in verse 4...is emphatic, meaning, 'I prayed, and kept on praying.'" James cites Monica, Augustine's mother, as one of the "saints of old [with] much to teach us about the value of the long labor of prayer." Who has been or is a model for you of calling on God persistently and passionately? When was a time you persistently and passionately called on God in prayer? What happened?

- James says the Hebrew word for the "simple" whom God preserves (verse 6a) "implies the naive, the gullible, the vulnerable, and the helpless." When was a time you were "simple"? How were you preserved through that time? What "simple" person, if any, might say God has preserved them through you, and why?

- "So much American thinking is about taking care of ourselves." How do you see this tendency in your community and culture? How do we strike a healthy balance between caring for ourselves and trusting in God's care?

- James suggests God's will—seen in Creation (Genesis 2:2-3), in the Exodus (Exodus 20:8-11), and in Jesus (Matthew 11:28-30)—is to bring us to a state of rest. What is rest? How does rest differ, in James's words, from "laziness or doing nothing for God"? How, specifically, do you rest in God's goodness, as the psalmist does (verse 7)?

Near-Death Experiences

Discuss:

- What does the psalmist say about the experience that prompted him to call on God (verses 3-4, 6b, 8)? Why do you think he doesn't describe this experience in more detail?

- James tells about a time he was near death. Have you ever had a similar experience? If so, how has your experience of "having made it when [you] might not have" affected your life since?

- "You, I, and everybody else are near death all day, every day." In what ways are you aware of being "near death" each day? What impact, if any, does this awareness have on how you go about your days "in the land of the living" (verse 9b)?

- James also describes "the death that settles upon and within us even while your heart is still beating and you're out and about." When, if ever, have you been aware of this kind of death? How did you or how do you deal with it?

- "The psalmist was 'saved,'" James states (verse 6b)—he lived on after having been "very close to death, physical or spiritual." How is this definition of "being saved" like or unlike what you think "being saved" means?

- The psalmist affirms he "kept [his] faith" even when "greatly afflicted" and hopeless (verses 10-11). Whom do you know or know of who has kept their faith when near death, in any of its forms?

How Much Do I Owe You?

Recruit a volunteer to read aloud Matthew 26:26-30. Discuss:

- Read Genesis 35:9-15; Numbers 15:5-10; Leviticus 23:9-14; 2 Samuel 23:13-17. What do drink offerings in the Old Testament signify? How is the psalmist's declaration in Psalm 116:12-13 like and unlike these drink offerings?

- How is Jesus's thanksgiving over the cup at the Last Supper like and unlike the psalmist's drink offering?

- How is your congregation's celebration of Holy Communion (or the Lord's Supper, or Eucharist—which means "thanksgiving") a declaration of thanksgiving and love to God?

- Have you ever sworn a vow to God, as the psalmist does (verses 14, 18)? If so, did you keep it? If not, would you consider swearing such a vow? Why or why not?

Precious in the Sight of the Lord

Discuss:

- What does the psalmist mean when he calls the death of God's saints "precious" in God's sight (verse 15)?
- James says the Hebrew word translated "precious" can also mean "costly." How does this translation influence your understanding of the verse?
- What is the costliest death you have personally experienced? How do you respond to the idea that, as James states, "God is in solidarity with us, the divine heart aching with sorrow"?
- Have you ever experienced, as James says many people he knows have, "a beauty, a tenderness, a wonder" at the time of someone's death?
- James notes the word translated "saint" "doesn't mean an officially sanctioned saint" but "the loyal, devoted follower, the one who prays, seeks God, tries their best, believes, and in extremity knows of nothing else to do but to place life themself into God's strong, loving hands." Who do you know or know of whom you would call a "saint" by this definition? Why?
- James calls verse 15 "the psalm's (and all of Scripture's) climax." Why? Do you agree with him? Why or why not?

Closing Your Session: Practicing God's Language for Prayer

Thank the group members for their presence and participation in this study of *The Heart of the Psalms*. Ask volunteers to talk briefly about one thing they will most remember, one question they still have, or one idea from the study they would like to share with others.

Remind participants that in his introduction, James talks about the Psalms teaching us God's language for prayer. Lead them in brainstorming a list of words, phrases, or images they remember from the psalms they have studied together. Write their responses on newsprint or markerboard.

Distribute scrap paper. Invite participants to choose one or two of these words, phrases, or images and to write one or more new psalm-like verses using it or inspired by it or them. Allow time for volunteers to share their verses. Be ready to share your own!

Closing Prayer

Sing or read together "I'll Praise My Maker" (*The United Methodist Hymnal* 60; https://hymnary.org/text/ill_praise_my_maker_with_my _breath) or some other hymn or song based on or inspired by Psalm 116.

Watch videos based on *The Heart of the Psalms* with Jame C. Howell through Amplify Media.

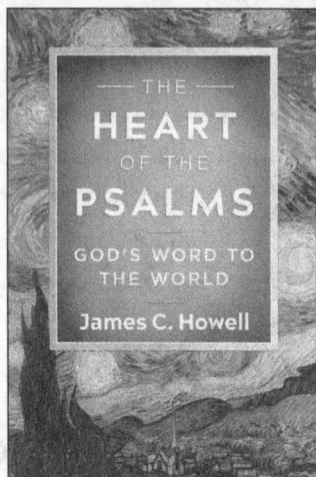

Amplify Media is a multimedia platform that delivers high-quality, searchable content with an emphasis on Wesleyan perspectives for churchwide, group, or individual use on any device at any time. In a world of sometimes overwhelming choices, Amplify gives church leaders and congregants media capabilities that are contemporary, relevant, effective and, most important, affordable and sustainable.

With *Amplify Media* church leaders can:

- Provide a reliable source of Christian content through a Wesleyan lens for teaching, training, and inspiration in a customizable library
- Deliver their own preaching and worship content in a way the congregation knows and appreciates
- Build the church's capacity to innovate with engaging content and accessible technology
- Equip the congregation to better understand the Bible and its application
- Deepen discipleship beyond the church walls

⋀ AMPLIFY™ MEDIA

Ask your group leader or pastor about Amplify Media and sign up today at www.AmplifyMedia.com.